MG 7.1 lpt.

ALL
ABOUT **SPACE
SCIENCE**

JOURNEY TO MARS

David Baker and
Heather Kissock

MEDIA ENHANCED BOOKS
AV²
BY WEIGL
ADDED VALUE • AUDIO VISUAL

www.av2books.com

AV² provides enriched content that supplements and complements this book. Weigl's AV² books strive to create inspired learning and engage young minds in a total learning experience.

Your AV² Media Enhanced books come alive with...

Audio
Listen to sections of the book read aloud.

Key Words
Study vocabulary, and complete a matching word activity.

Video
Watch informative video clips.

Quizzes
Test your knowledge.

Go to **www.av2books.com**, and enter this book's unique code.

Embedded Weblinks
Gain additional information for research.

Slide Show
View images and captions, and prepare a presentation.

BOOK CODE

P442884

Try This!
Complete activities and hands-on experiments.

... and much, much more!

AV² by Weigl brings you media enhanced books that support active learning.

Published by AV² by Weigl
350 5th Avenue, 59th Floor
New York, NY 10118
Website: www.av2books.com

Library of Congress Cataloging-in-Publication Data

Names: Baker, David, 1944- author. | Kissock, Heather, author.
Title: Journey to Mars / David Baker, Heather Kissock.
Description: New York, NY : AV2 by Weigl, 2017. | Series: All about space
 science | Includes index.
Identifiers: LCCN 2016054641 (print) | LCCN 2017002320 (ebook) | ISBN
 9781489658272 (hard cover : alk. paper) | ISBN 9781489658289 (soft cover :
 alk. paper) | ISBN 9781489658296 (Multi-user ebk.)
Subjects: LCSH: Mars (Planet)--Exploration--Juvenile literature.
Classification: LCC QB641 .B228 2017 (print) | LCC QB641 (ebook) | DDC
 523.43--dc23
LC record available at https://lccn.loc.gov/2016054641

Printed in the United States of America in Brainerd, Minnesota
1 2 3 4 5 6 7 8 9 0 21 20 19 18 17

032017
020117

Editor: Katie Gillespie
Art Director: Terry Paulhus

Photo Credits
Every reasonable effort has been made to trace ownership and to obtain permission to reprint copyright material. The publishers would be pleased to have any errors or omissions brought to their attention so that they may be corrected in subsequent printings.

Weigl acknowledges Getty Images, iStock, Alamy, Shutterstock, and NASA as its primary image suppliers for this title.

ALL ABOUT SPACE SCIENCE

JOURNEY TO MARS

CONTENTS

The Fourth Planet

On a cloudless night, the planet Mars can be seen clearly with the naked eye. It appears as a reddish light, shining like a bright star. Mars is sometimes called the "red planet" because of its reddish hue.

Mars is the fourth planet from the Sun. After Venus, it is the planet closest to Earth. During its **orbit**, Mars comes within 35 million miles (56 million kilometers) of Earth. Mars is much smaller than Earth in size, but the two planets share many traits. In fact, scientists believe that, at one time, Mars had a similar environment to Earth.

Mars appears larger in the night sky when its orbit brings it closer to Earth. In 2016, Mars looked bigger in May, and smaller in January and December.

Its closeness to Earth has encouraged many theories about what Mars is like. People through time have held the belief that the planet was home to living beings. This belief was promoted by many science fiction writers, who created an imaginary world inhabited by beings called Martians. Authors such as H.G. Wells, Edgar Rice Burroughs, and Ray Bradbury created stories about these space aliens. As space technology developed, these stories were proven to be baseless.

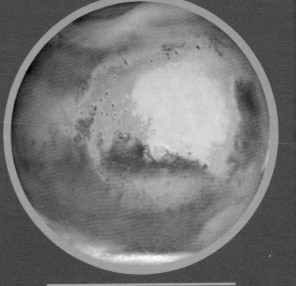

Although Mars is half the size of Earth, it has about the same land area. This is because Mars does not have oceans.

Scientists have not yet found evidence of life on Mars. Still, the idea that there could be life there encouraged scientists to find ways to get close to the planet and even to land on it. As a result, Mars is one of the most explored planets in the **solar system**.

THE RED PLANET

From a distance, the planet Mars looks red. This is because Mars has a great deal of **iron oxide** in its surface dust. In most places, this layer of dust is actually very thin. The dirt underneath the top layer is brown.

If an astronaut stood on Mars and looked up, the sky would also look red to him or her. This effect is created by dust in the air that scatters the sunlight in a particular way. Sunsets on Mars, however, appear to be blue in color.

A Planet of Interest

Human fascination with Mars began many centuries ago. Probably because of its reddish color, an ancient people called the Babylonians named it Nergal, after the god of fire and destruction. Its modern name of Mars came from the Romans, who named it after their god of war.

Mars has two **moons named Phobos and Deimos.**

Since the invention of the telescope in 1609, scientists have been looking at Mars in more detail. One feature they noticed early in their studies was a series of straight lines running over the planet's surface. The scientists of the time believed that these lines were **irrigation canals**. They thought that beings similar to humans must have lived on Mars and built the structures.

Valles Marineris is a canyon on Mars. At 1,864 miles (3,000 km) long, 311 miles (500 km) wide, and 5 miles (8 km) deep, it is the largest canyon in the solar system.

Scientists also saw light and dark patches move across the surface of the planet. Some scientists believed that these were seasonal changes, like those that occur on Earth. Other scientists thought these patches were plants that grew in the spring and died in the fall. They suggested that the plants were being grown by living beings, who would sow seeds in the spring and harvest crops in the summer. This theory promoted the idea that life existed on Mars.

As a result, Mars became a priority destination when space travel first became possible. After the first probe successfully reached the Moon, scientists focused their attention on the red planet. The first probe was sent to Mars in 1964. Since then, at least 20 other spacecraft have successfully reached the planet, and more continue to be scheduled. While it is uncertain if Mars ever held life, scientists want to know if living beings could survive there today.

The first probe sent to Mars cost **$83.2 million.**

Many artists have envisioned what a colony on Mars might look like, including the kinds of houses, vehicles, and clothing that would suit the planet's harsh environment.

Mars Explorers

Humans have yet to step on Mars. Instead, scientists have sent a variety of spacecraft to the planet to take pictures and run tests. These spacecraft include three types of space probes and a robotic vehicle called a rover.

FLYBY PROBE
Flyby probes take readings and pictures of space bodies as they fly past them. These probes only study the space body for a few hours and usually only focus on one area.

ORBITER PROBE
An orbiter probe stays with the planet for a longer period. It orbits, or circles, the body, taking pictures and readings of the area the orbit covers.

LANDER PROBE

Lander probes actually touch down on the planet or space body. This allows for more detailed research on the environment. Landers stay in the place where they landed for their entire mission.

ROVER

Rovers are vehicles brought to a space body by a lander probe. The lander probe releases them, and they then travel over the terrain of the body. They can then gather detailed information about different parts of the planet or space body.

LANDING ROVERS ON MARS

To land rovers on Mars, spacecraft need to decelerate from a velocity of about 13,200 miles (21,243 km) per hour. A spacecraft's first brake is its heatshield. Once the heatshield is discarded, a large parachute opens. The spacecraft then blasts braking rockets to further slow its descent. Some spacecraft then lower their rover down to the surface on lines. Others release their rover covered in protective materials. It takes about seven minutes to land a spacecraft on Mars.

Touchdown on Mars

In 1975, **NASA** sent two probes, *Viking 1* and *2*, to Mars. The mission of these orbiters was to circle the planet and take pictures. Attached to each orbiter was another part called a lander. Its mission was to detach from the orbiter and set down on the planet.

The two *Viking* landers touched down on different parts of Mars. *Viking 1* landed in an area called Chryse Planitia, near a large canyon. This was where scientists thought there might have been shallow seas at one time. They were hopeful that **fossils** of ancient life forms might be found. *Viking 2* landed on the other side of Mars. Here, the surface was strewn with rocks spewed by volcanoes long ago. Each lander carried a set of instruments to test soil samples for signs of life, but none were found. The landers were only expected to work for six months, but both lasted much longer. *Viking 2* worked for five years. *Viking 1* stopped working after seven years.

NASA planned *Viking 1*'s landing spot using photos from the orbiter probe *Mariner 9*'s trip to Mars. Once *Viking 1* got close to Mars and sent clearer images back to Earth, NASA changed the landing spot to a safer, flatter area.

Both *Viking* probes were launched on a Titan rocket from Cape Canaveral, Florida.

The Titan 111-E rocket that launched the *Viking* probes had two strap-on rockets to provide extra boost at liftoff.

A New Plan

During the 1980s, scientists were eager to send more spacecraft to Mars. However, as more parts were added to probes, the cost of making them and sending them into space increased. NASA could not afford to continue the missions as they were.

Scientists and engineers worked together to produce a new type of spacecraft that could be faster, better, and cheaper than those of the past. They used modern computers and technology to reduce the size and weight of each spacecraft and increase the amount of information they could send back.

In 1996, NASA sent two probes to Mars as part of this new program. One, called Mars Global Surveyor, entered Mars' orbit and took pictures of the surface. These would be used to map the planet over several years.

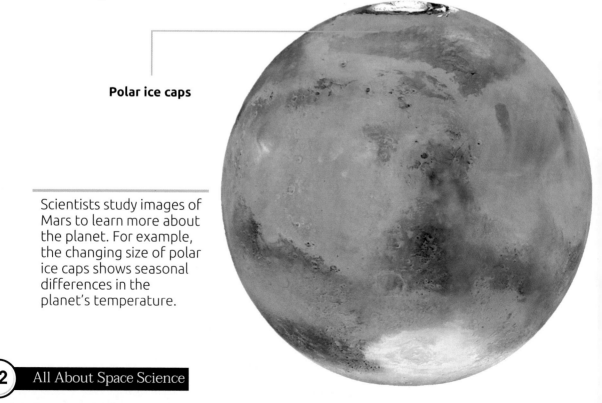

Polar ice caps

Scientists study images of Mars to learn more about the planet. For example, the changing size of polar ice caps shows seasonal differences in the planet's temperature.

To reduce the amount of fuel needed to operate Mars Global Surveyor, scientists added a small braking rocket. Instead of using fuel to move into position, the probe used the **gravity** of Mars to pull it into orbit. As Surveyor sliced through Mars' **atmosphere**, the brake slowed the probe and gently lowered it into orbit. This technique is known as aerobraking.

The second spacecraft launched was Mars Pathfinder. Pathfinder was built as a lander probe. It was meant to land on Mars and gather information from the planet's surface. In the past, lander probes had been very expensive to operate. Many of them did not make successful landings, and were damaged or destroyed during the process. This added to the cost of the mission. To increase the chance of a safe landing, NASA's scientists attached airbags to the probe. This helped to prevent the vehicle from being damaged, and it reduced the amount of fuel needed to control the probe's braking rockets.

Olympus Mons on Mars is the **tallest mountain** in the **solar system**.

Mars has the **LARGEST dust storms** in the **solar system**.

Once Mars Pathfinder safely landed, it deflated and retracted its airbags.

The Little Rover that Could

The exploration of Mars could only really begin when robot spacecraft could land on the surface and move around. The orbiting spacecraft circling Mars had revealed much that scientists did not know about the planet. However, the closest look of all, from the surface, was the only way to get detailed information about conditions on the planet. *Viking 1* and *Viking 2* had landed on Mars in 1976, but they had stayed in specific locations on the planet. As a result, they were only able to give scientists information about those places.

When Mars Pathfinder landed on Mars in 1997, a new age in Mars exploration began. Pathfinder was actually two vehicles. Inside the lander was a small rover, called Sojourner. Sojourner's ability to move over the planet's surface allowed scientists to explore new places. The rover gathered information from different parts of the planet. This increased scientists' understanding of the planet's geology and the materials that form its surface.

Sojourner's mission on Mars only lasted for three months. In that time, it sent 550 images of the planet to Earth. These images suggested that, at one time, Mars had a warm, moist climate.

Sojourner's maximum speed was about 0.4 inches (1 centimeter) per second.

ROVER POWER

Sojourner was powered mainly by electricity produced from **solar cells**. This power operated the rover's motor and its communications system, which allowed scientists on Earth to send and receive information via radio signals. Using solar power limited the places on Mars that Sojourner could explore. The rover needed to land and stay in an area that received plenty of sunlight. Modern rovers use plutonium as a source of power. They can explore areas that receive less sunlight without running out of energy.

Sojourner weighed only 23 pounds (11 kilograms).

A Renewed Interest

The success of Sojourner led to the creation of more Mars rovers. In June and July 2003, NASA launched two rovers, Spirit and Opportunity. Each one was bigger, and designed to last longer, than the little Sojourner rover launched in 1996.

Called robotic geologists, the rovers' job was to research the history of water on Mars. Spirit landed on Mars in a crater called Gusev. Scientists believe that Gusev may have been a lake at one time. Opportunity landed on the opposite side of Mars in a place called Meridiani Planum. Here, **mineral deposits** show that Mars had once been a moist planet.

Each rover was equipped with special instruments that could examine rocks and other materials on the planet's surface. One instrument measured the **chemical composition** of surface rocks. A robotic arm allowed the rover to pick up rocks.

Spirit stopped communicating with Earth in 2010. Opportunity continues to perform research. Both have shown scientists that Mars once had plenty of liquid water.

In 2015, NASA announced it had observed flowing rivers of salt water on Mars.

The Mars Phoenix landing probe set down on the northern polar region of Mars in May 2008. It was sent to study the polar ice, as well as collect information on the planet's weather. Phoenix discovered that Mars receives snowfall. This shows moisture in the atmosphere.

Another probe, the Mars Reconnaissance Orbiter, carried **radar** equipment to study beneath Mars' surface. Underneath many layers of rock, the probe found several huge **glaciers**. These glaciers could provide humans with a water source if they land on Mars. They may also contain fossils of life forms that once lived on the planet.

In 2012, the rover Curiosity landed on Mars. Its mission was to determine if life could have survived on Mars, and if the planet could be habitable in the future. During its first year, Curiosity found carbon, hydrogen, oxygen, phosphorus, and sulfur. These are key ingredients for life. Curiosity continues to study Mars and report back to Earth.

Curiosity carries a laser that can remove a thin layer from a rock and analyze its composition.

Making the Grade

Working with space probes and rovers requires people to have very specific skills and education. Probe and rover specialists must have a good grasp of science principles, along with strong technical skills. They must be detail-oriented people who strive to improve current technologies. With these traits and qualifications, there are many career paths that can be taken.

ASTRONAUT QUALIFICATIONS

CITIZENSHIP
Pilots and **mission specialists** must be U.S. citizens. **Payload specialists** can be from other countries.

HEIGHT
Pilots must be 62 to 75 inches (157.5 to 190.5 centimeters) tall. Mission or payload specialists must be 58.5 to 76 inches (148.5 to 193 cm) tall.

HEALTH
All astronauts must pass a NASA physical, with specific vision and blood pressure requirements.

EXPERIENCE
Astronauts must have at least three years of experience in a science-related field. Pilots must have jet experience with more than 1,000 hours of in-command flight time.

EDUCATION
Astronauts must have a minimum bachelor's degree in engineering, biology, physics, or mathematics. Most astronauts have a **doctorate**.

ASTRONAUTICAL ENGINEER Astronautical engineers design, develop, and test spacecraft, including probes and rovers. They often specialize in very specific areas, such as structural design and navigation or communication systems. It is their job to create equipment and vehicles that can survive the journey from Earth to space and back again. They need to have expert knowledge on the conditions the equipment will experience so that the correct materials and technology are used to create it. They are involved in the construction process from design to finished product.

SOFTWARE ENGINEER Software engineers make computer programs that operate inside the probes and rovers. These programs may help with the vehicle's navigation system or with the work that the vehicle is in space to do, such as measure magnetic fields and take soil samples. Once these programs are developed, the software engineer will make sure that they work properly, testing them from time to time, and correcting any parts of the program that are not working well.

LAUNCH MANAGER A launch manager is the person who prepares to launch a probe or rover into space. Launch managers schedule the launch process. The launch manager arranges for a launch vehicle, such as a rocket or space shuttle, to carry the probe into space. Launch managers arrange to transport the probe to the launch site. They must have a good understanding of the probe development process, as well as NASA's safety standards, so that the launch process runs smoothly and safely.

New Ways to Explore

While probes and rovers have been exploring Mars, scientists have been developing new technology to take the research even further. Scientists are currently working on plans to use airplanes in their study of the red planet. The airplane they are designing will not carry people. Instead, it will have its own **navigation** system, so it can steer itself around Mars. Scientists believe that airplanes will be able to gather more information about Mars than rovers and probes. They can fly closer to the surface than an orbiter probe and cover more area than a rover.

An airplane could carry a camera and take closeup photos of the Mars landscape as it flies.

HELICOPTERS ON MARS

NASA scientists are experimenting with a drone-like helicopter they hope to send to Mars. The helicopter is roughly the size of a tissue box, and weighs about 2.2 pounds (1 kg). It can fly for a few minutes at a time.

Scientists hope this tiny helicopter will be able to fly ahead of a rover and scout out the best route for the rover to take. This would save time in planning routes. Scientists estimate that using the helicopter could allow the rover to cover up to three times more territory each day.

NASA scientists are also planning to send equipment to Mars that can explore the planet's subsurface. They have developed a 130-foot (40-meter) antenna that uses radar to detect and map underground water. The radar waves will be able to find water as deep as 3 miles (5 km) below the surface of Mars.

Scientists have also developed robotic moles. These moles will be able to drill deep into the planet's surface, gathering soil samples at each stage of their journey. These samples will be sent to the surface using a long tube. Once at the surface, the samples will be analyzed by special **imaging** equipment to see what minerals are available underground.

Currently, there is no way to bring the samples back to Earth for further study. Scientists are working on making rockets that could go to and from Mars for this purpose. They are also developing containers that will protect the samples from contamination and damage.

A Day in Space

Space probes and other vehicles are often taken into space by a space shuttle. When a shuttle takes a probe into space, releasing it is just one job in a day that has a firmly set schedule, with certain tasks to be done at specific times. Flight controllers on Earth wake up the crew in the morning with a pop song that they blast over the shuttle's speakers. After eating breakfast, it is time for the astronauts to get ready for work.

A list, known as the flight plan, tells the crew what they are to work on each day. Sometimes, there is the need for a spacewalk. Other times, the crew carries out housekeeping duties, such as trash collection and cleaning. Breaks, such as lunch and dinner, are scheduled throughout the day. Blocks of time are put aside for the astronauts to set up and use exercise equipment. At the end of the work day, the astronauts may read a book, listen to music, watch a movie, or check emails.

Astronaut candidates undergo testing for up to two years before qualifying for a mission. Many of these tests focus on how they work as part of team.

THE DAILY SCHEDULE

8:30 to 10:00 a.m.
Post-sleep (Morning station inspection, breakfast, morning **hygiene**)

1.5 hours

10:00 to 10:30 a.m.
Planning and coordination (Daily planning conference and status report)

0.5 hours

2.5 hours
10:30 a.m. to 1:00 p.m.
Exercise (Set up exercise equipment, exercise, and put equipment away)

1.0 hours
1:00 to 2:00 p.m.
Lunch, personal hygiene

2:00 to 3:30 p.m.
Daily systems operations (Work preparation, report writing, emails, to-do list review, trash collection)

1.5 hours

3:30 to 10:00 p.m.
Work (Work set-up and maintenance, performing experiments and payload operations, checking positioning and operating systems)

6.5 hours

10:00 p.m. to 12:00 a.m.
Pre-sleep (Food preparation, evening meal, and hygiene)

2.0 hours

8.5 hours
12:00 to 8:30 a.m.
Sleep

Footprints on Mars

The ultimate goal of NASA's Mars Exploration Program is to put humans on the planet. Currently, NASA, the Russian Space Agency, and the **European Space Agency** are all planning to send people to Mars. It is estimated that this will occur in the 2030s.

Before people can land on Mars, scientists must be able to ensure their safety. One of the main concerns scientists have about Mars is the level of **radiation** found there. Unlike Earth, Mars does not have an ozone layer to protect it from the Sun's **ultraviolet rays**. Before humans can go to Mars, scientists must determine how much radiation Mars receives and design spacesuits and other equipment to counter it.

Deserts on Earth are similar to the surface on Mars. They provide good training grounds for future astronauts.

The mission to Mars will take about 12 to 18 months. During the journey and while on Mars, astronauts will need food, water, air, and shelter. Scientists are researching how to meet these needs. They are learning how to recycle water and grow food in space. They are designing new machines that will mine water, oxygen, and hydrogen from the soil on Mars. They are also testing other machines, such as 3D printers, that could help provide shelter and tools on Mars.

Once all the studies have taken place and the proper equipment created, human missions will begin taking place. The first missions will be for short periods. Over time, however, scientists hope to build a research station on Mars. Astronauts will stay on the planet for longer periods and perform more in-depth research and experiments.

NASA scientists test habitats and equipment at Black Point Lava Flow in Arizona.

Early Exploration

The exploration of Mars began in 1964 when scientists sent probes to the red planet. For the next eight years, different probes took photos of Mars and sent them back to Earth. This timeline highlights the probe missions that formed the basis of all further exploration of the planet.

November 1964 The first spacecraft sent to Mars was launched. It was a NASA probe called *Mariner 4*.

July 1965 *Mariner 4* flew by Mars. As it did, it took 22 black and white pictures, which were sent back to Earth. The pictures proved that the planet did not have **extraterrestrial beings** living on it. Instead, the pictures showed Mars to have a barren, sandy landscape covered with craters. The canals that early scientists thought they had seen were an optical illusion. Still, *Mariner*'s pictures indicated that water did flow on the planet at one time.

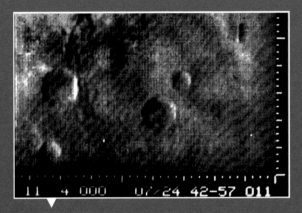

1969 NASA probes *Mariners 6* and *7* successfully launched and, like *Mariner 4*, flew past Mars, taking hundreds of pictures of the red planet. However, these missions only provided a brief glimpse of the planet.

THE FACE ON MARS

Children often play shadow puppets with their hands on a wall lit by candles. Light can play tricks with the imagination. This occurred during the *Viking* missions to Mars.

One of the *Viking* orbiters sent back a picture of an object that looked like a human face. Some people believed that it was a sculpture carved by an ancient Martian civilization. NASA received thousands of letters from people wanting the space agency to investigate.

Later, other spacecraft took pictures over the same area. These spacecraft had better cameras that took clearer photos. When people examined the images it was almost impossible to see any likeness to a human face. The effects of shadow and light had changed the look of the landscape, making it appear to be something that was not there. The photos showed that the face was actually a mesa, similar to those found in the American West.

1971 *Mariner 8* and *Mariner 9* were launched. *Mariner 8*'s main engine shut down 365 seconds after launch, and the probe fell into the Atlantic Ocean. *Mariner 9* launched successfully. This probe was an orbiter. When it reached Mars, it became the first probe to set a course around the planet. For almost one year, it circled the planet twice a day, taking thousands of pictures of seasonal changes and surface details.

1972 *Mariner 9* found that the planet's North and South Poles were covered with ice. The probe did not find liquid water, but it took pictures of land formations that looked like riverbeds. This indicated that, at one time, water had flowed on the planet. As water is key to life, this discovery again raised the question about life on Mars.

Mariner 9 was the first spacecraft to orbit another planet.

The area where the mesa lies is named Cydonia. This area has many mesas. Even though the face-like mesa is not an alien-made sculpture, it and other nearby mesas are still of interest to scientists because they are in a transition zone. To the south of the mesas are highlands, and to the north is a plain thought to have once been an ocean.

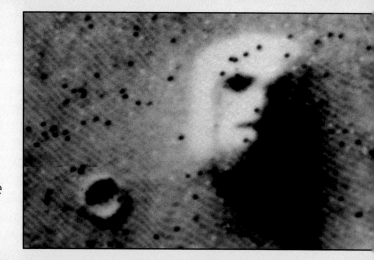

Journey to Mars Quiz

1

What color is Mars?

2

Which space vehicle can travel over the terrain of a planet?

3

In what year was the telescope invented?

4

What was the name of the first probe to orbit another planet?

5

What special feature on Pathfinder helped it to land safely?

6 Where did Viking 1 land?

7 How long would a mission to Mars take?

8 What key ingredients for life did Curiosity find on Mars?

9 How long do astronauts exercise for every day?

10 What is an astronaut's daily activity list called?

Key Words

atmosphere: the layer of gases that surrounds Earth

chemical composition: the substances that make up an object

doctorate: an advanced university degree

European Space Agency: an organization formed to develop Europe's space capabilities

extraterrestrial beings: life forms that do not originate on Earth

fossils: the remains of organisms from the past

glaciers: slow-moving sheets of ice

gravity: a force that pulls things toward each other

hygiene: the process of keeping clean

imaging: the process of creating pictures

iron oxide: a naturally occurring substance that is red in color

irrigation canals: manmade channels used to transport water

mineral deposits: masses of naturally occurring rocks and ores

mission specialists: scientists sent into space by NASA

NASA: National Aeronautics and Space Administration; the United States' civilian agency for research into space and aviation

navigation: the act of directing or plotting a path

orbit: the path a satellite or other spacecraft travels around a planet or other space object

payload specialists: scientists sent into space by companies or countries other than the United States

radar: an electronic instrument that uses radio waves to find the distance and location of other objects

radiation: energy given off in the form of waves or very tiny particles

solar cells: devices that convert the energy of sunlight into electric energy

solar system: the Sun together with the eight planets and all other bodies that orbit the Sun

ultraviolet rays: invisible beams of light that are part of the energy that comes from the Sun

Index

Log on to www.av2books.com

AV² by Weigl brings you media enhanced books that support active learning. Go to www.av2books.com, and enter the special code found on page 2 of this book. You will gain access to enriched and enhanced content that supplements and complements this book. Content includes video, audio, weblinks, quizzes, a slide show, and activities.

AV² Online Navigation

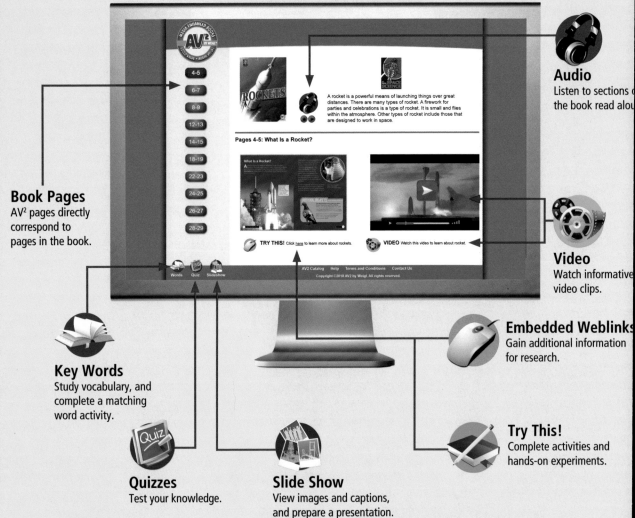

Book Pages
AV² pages directly correspond to pages in the book.

Audio
Listen to sections of the book read alou

Video
Watch informative video clips.

Embedded Weblinks
Gain additional information for research.

Key Words
Study vocabulary, and complete a matching word activity.

Try This!
Complete activities and hands-on experiments.

Quizzes
Test your knowledge.

Slide Show
View images and captions, and prepare a presentation.

AV² was built to bridge the gap between print and digital. We encourage you to tell us what you like and what you want to see in the future.

Sign up to be an AV² Ambassador at www.av2books.com/ambassador.